Xueyan's exceptional poetry col[lection] *Original White* combines brillia[nt] structures and original ideas.

With poems that are both imaginative and erudite, this book encompasses questions of perennial concern. It often dissects such questions in modern settings and with contemporary language. Its topics include the nature of God, the existence of evil, the brutality of capitalism, the loneliness of existence, and the reach of human love. Each entry is brief; some are composed of just a few lines. Each word counts in these poems, including their titles, which are often essential to comprehension. Still, entire worlds exist in these jewel boxes because of their precise linguistic turns, clever line breaks, and uses of alliteration and assonance.

Astonishing juxtapositions result in compelling arguments for a cosmopolitan world view. In the three-line entry "Office Building," "Living corpses sit and stare / Company epitaph is composed of their names." And in intellectually pleasing entries concerned with the human condition, paradoxes and irony expose people's frailty, as with the irony of the human drive for conquest that comes into sharp relief in "Big Small":

> Even if I have conquered the whole world
> after death
> my body will rest in only one tiny plot.

In other entries, a more visceral kind of pleasure is available. There are startling and impactful images present throughout: in "Color of Sin," "Eve bites the apple / It begins to oxidize." It's a singular take on a familiar scene, operating in an organic fashion within the entry's concise, balanced form.

While elements of Buddhism and classical mythology inform some entries, most of the poems that are concerned with the nature of God are framed in a structure of Christian imagery and biblical traditions. This is accomplished with reverence, impudence, or both, revealing the complexity of belief. Human sensuality competes with faith for primacy in poems where "Flesh entangles / the two planks of a cross / our bodies nailed / bleeding yet blazing," reversing the usual hierarchy of spirit over flesh. Here, there is room for both desire and holiness. Vigorous lines take on the power of God by claiming the identity of "fire / fire / fire / the waving skirt of Joan of Arc / the thorny crown of Jesus Christ."

Inventive, beautiful, and deep, the poems of *Time Peels All to Original White* beg to be read again and again.

—*Foreword Clarion Reviews*

Dedicated to "beautiful souls swallowed by darkness," this striking collection from Xueyan joins sharply sculpted lines, a penchant for emotionally charged descriptions of nature and divinity, an urgent longing for connection, and a reverence for Christ, whom the poet imagines, in a verse of rhapsodic transformation, first carrying the poet "along the thorny path of blood and flame" while Xueyan is a butterfly on his holy shoulders. A poem like "Valley of the Shadow of Death" unites theme, form, and language: "Answer me: / Where is the valley of the shadow of death? // Is it in the shade /beneath the eternal suffering of the cross? // Or is it within the wrinkles of my mother's face?"

The short, stinging "Cup," meanwhile, suggests that love—which in many poems is a redemptive force linked to eternity—can at times feel in short supply: "You empty my cup / by filling / hers." Xueyan wastes no words in these crisp, pared-down poems, though they're not short on meaning, mystery, or power. The biblical themes often connect to ideas of perseverance, as "John the Divine" finds in the life of the Baptist of the Gospels the lesson "Passion as paddle / belief as boat." "Parting: A Red Sea Love Story" at first seems tragicomic, as two fish who have fallen for each other are torn apart as a consequence of Moses's parting of the Red Sea. But the final lines offer a haunting evocation of a love that endures.

Another potent theme is that of exile. "Wind" reveals its subject as ancient, the "howl of Adam and Eve," expelled from the Garden, while "Strangers," "You Did Not," and other poems about lost or fleeting connection pack maximal feeling into a minimum of words. The sacred, the eternal, the ecstasy of intimacy: Xueyan binds all this together, in tight, gripping verse, writing "Every fleeting moment / we breathe and create together / is eternity."

—*BookLife* by *Publishers Weekly*

A Chinese poet seeks answers in the sky and the soul in this debut collection.

This is not a book for the casual poetry fan; from the first page to the last, the poems are dramatic and deeply spiritual. "Breaking free from waves of sorrows / I leap ashore / Stars coronate me / beads of tears on hairs ribboned by light / I am owned by eternity," writes Xueyan in her collection's closing work and author's note. The collection's nearly 140 concise poems, arranged in four parts, dwell mostly on the nature of human devotion, the heavens, and the machinations of God, and they do not provide answers. Many entries reflect on mortality, painting humanity's sacrifices with macabre strokes; in "Prophet," Xueyan writes, "The halo hangs above me / a holy gallows / Enchanted by light / I ascend to the aureole / to the sacred execution of my mortal flesh / My eyes / my skin / my tongue / melt." This abundance of unsettling descriptions, while compelling, occasionally overshadows the poems' meaning. Other entries consider the lessons of Greek myths ("Prometheus's Fire," "Icarus"), the Bible ("Lilith Leaves Eden," "The Crucifixion"), and religious history ("Jerusalem").

Xueyan reverently explores Mary and Christ as tragic figures, and the imagery can be stark and memorable. The poet seems to suggest that brutality is cyclic and inevitable; snow and water appear again and again to signal both beauty and death. Poems on romance also address God: "A tear shed for love / is deeper than the sea / When I murmur your name to the winds / I am as clean as Yahweh's bones." Xueyan adroitly explores her themes, but not all of the poems feel necessary, and some of the shortest ones simply retrace what has already been expressed. Despite an overall somber tone, she finds occasional moments of levity: "After long journeys / two fish finally meet / love at first sight / They are going to kiss." The closing section departs somewhat from the cosmic framing of the majority of the works and incorporates more mundane language; cigarettes, electricity bills, and the subway add grounded contrast with natural beauty and Messianic references, but they don't always effectively mesh with the book's more ethereal scope. Some poems fewer than ten words ("Shortest Poem" simply says "Love") don't always justify their brevity, but the abrupt ends evoke the speaker's restlessness. Part of the book's intrigue lies in the author's opacity and lack of personal details. The closing poem, "To Wake," does the best job of distilling the poet's seeming intended takeaway for her readers about the dissonance of Christian aspirations compared with the burden of everyday life: "Humans wake because they are hungry / not because they love the world."

Ably and originally muses on Christianity and personal sacrifice.

—*Kirkus Reviews*

Time Peels All
to Original White

Xueyan Poems

Fernwood
PRESS

Time Peels All to Original White

Fernwood Press
Newberg, Oregon
https://www.fernwoodpress.com

Printed in the United States of America

Cover and page design: Mareesa Fawver Moss

ISBN 978-1-59498-092-3

Library of Congress Control Number: 2022942382

For beautiful souls swallowed by darkness

Author's Bio-Poem

Xueyan

A mirage imprisoned in dew

a shadow of the Ultimate's dream—

when my heart stops whispering to the abyss
and embraces the flame of the Divine

snow will fall
the bone ashes of a star

Contents

Part I

Every blink is lightning

The Color of Eyes
Is the Color of Soul

Time peels all
to original white

but the color of eyes remains

Yours
black butterfly slumbers on snow

dreaming of moonlight

Tower of Babel

We entangle

White tower spirals from our spine

until it interlocks with the eternal gaze of God

Even though we can dream
        the galactic eyes of the Divine

our bones still sting like snow

Secret of Heart

I lean my head against thy chest
through the starry boundlessness within
The heart named eternity whispers

From the holy grail, emptiness is spilling
Lord's oracular lips are forever silent
I rise as abyss and fall as fate

Paradise Lost

A twig waves in wind
reaching out to the moon in vain
a tired hand
yearning for eternity

A bird with no song
lies in the street
deserted by life and by death

Hurricane blown by an angel
spreads its wings to

abandon heaven

An Angel's Elegy

Death flows over me
like water on rock

Heaven's wings are not snow
but heaviest gravestone

Only carrying death can I soar

H

Already dead, I am

living my afterlife

here

in the form of

human

Big Small

Even if I have conquered the whole world

after death

my body will rest in only one tiny plot

Three Souls of the Sea

One elopes with the sky and becomes cloud

One yearns to hear the singing of birds
    sneaks onto the land on a shell
        and becomes mountain

One remains wave after wave, breaking against the shore in
    everlasting moonlight sorrow

Color of Sin

Eve bites the apple

It begins to oxidize

Prophet

The halo hangs above me
a holy gallows
Enchanted by light
I ascend to the aureole
to the sacred execution of my mortal flesh
My eyes
my skin
my tongue
melt

Sun falls into my left void
moon into my right
I see the Ultimate

Clouds dress me
I sense the Infinite

The Milky Way flows into my mouth
I am Oracle

Sacrifice for Truth

To hold the fire

a candle

must melt

Why Are Saints in
This Sinful World

The night sky is dark

so the stars can shine

Oracle

To transcend sin
we must abandon salvation

To transcend ephemera
we must abandon eternity

Eternity through Ephemera

We must die

so

God can live

Crow

Crows hover above a coffin

The shadow of the corpse rises

and spreads its wings—

one more

Rustling When Counting

A tree stands alone
in the dark
counting its leaves

Every leaf when counted falls
one
two
three

The last number susurrated
wind sobs through barren limbs

My Pilgrimage to Nothingness

The abyss spreads shadowy wings

closes me

in the eye whites of God

Every blink is lightning

Death of a Poet

God loses a hair

Percy Bysshe Shelley falls into the sea

a string-severed marionette

Saint

The sea

knows all secrets

swallows all sounds

yet remains

silent for eternity

God Gazes

God has one eye
sun at day
moon at night

It does not blink
    as great kings pass
nor at the birth
    of a tiny trembling rose

Questions Destined for No Answers

Why does snow fall into this sinful world
    pure white?

Why do stars fade for the passing of the moon
    as though dying from love lost?

Why do we seek joy in life
    after entering the world with crying?

Joy

What dwells within a body?

A soul

What dwells within a soul?

A song

What dwells within a song?

Only sorrow

I dream of a land

where every heart when lonely dances

every petal when withers arrives at pearly gates

every tear becomes a star

Go

A toddler stumbles forward
falls into parent's arms

Years later, a bullet is shot

A soldier staggers backward
falls onto tyrant's ground

Bones

My tears turn to snow

falling inside me until I die

After a thousand years, my grave opens

In moonlight, my snow-tears glitter

World Ends Like Snow

The heavenly mirror

shatters

Shards fly shimmering

every piece an illusion

melting into

white

Cruel Truth

The world is unreal

or

the world is real

Humanity

When the goddess of night dons her black cloak
    and buttons up the stars

it is time for mortals
    to unbutton their desires

The crescent moon is the ethereal smile of the
    Divine

On my flesh, the same curve is gateway
    to pleasure and pain

That is why every baby is born
    with the soul of both angel and devil

Untitled

For us

God is unimaginable

vice versa

Balance

A coffin sinks

A belly swells

Existence

Glass broken

Silence born

Note: We are not aware of the existence of silence until a glass is broken; when all returns to silence, we notice it. Similarly, we are not aware of the wellness of our skin until it stings; when it heals, we notice it.

Secret

Every shadow

a veil to be lifted

a truth to be revealed

What lies beneath?

Fire

flood

another veil

The Real Abyss

I immerse myself in the abyss

The abyss is not abyss

I am abyss

Rule My World

I glare at the sun

until it cannot stand; it crashes

I close my eyes

The whole dark sky drops within

Theory of All

When Bathsheba appears naked as moonlight
King David sees his reflection
in the thousand water droplets on her skin

Giddy with power, he blurs
the boundary between saint and sinner, sets
aside some soldiers to procure
the once-human mirror
object of his hunger
He plunges into her

The flood from God engulfs him

Decades later
the king of wisdom sits on his lonely throne
a thousand women and not a drop of comfort:

I have seen it all, and it is all
as senseless as chasing the wind

Solomon listens to the void
the First Temple crumbling
Destined, he smiles

Hero

A hawk struck by lightning

felled and buried

until one day a barefoot saint treads upon it

Awoken by blood on scarred feet

soars as sword

knocks down the thorns-crown of night

Tree of Zion

In the Promised Land I dig a hole

bury my feet and take root

For years in silence I grow

I wait for the wind

to read the rings on my brow

Jerusalem

They wail against the wall

a tomb for the ancestors' displaced bones

When they with the bones weep

crying soars and slits the throat of the sun

Sunset blood floods their tearful eyes

Why We Must Suffer

Plucked

washed

cut

silent as ever

thrown into a boiling pot

moan bubbles

steam souls

gone

Prometheus's Fire

Prometheus flees Mount Olympus

on the tiger of roaring fire

He smites the stripes

Prison bars are broken

Fire wolfs down the darkness

山

First fire set
First eye of civilization opens

山

He Has an Apple

Slowly the old man pushed his cart
around the grocery

gathering cabbage, broccoli
an apple

That night he ate all but the apple

Morning found him curled on the sofa dead and cold
in his palm an apple with a dent

Did he gaze at it
like he gazed the first time he saw his mother's breast

Did he bite it
like the first time he joined lips with love

I don't know

but a long time ago a baby crawled up a giant umbrella
and pushed the apple button

The umbrella spread as did his life
all days and nights, all good and evil

Now God has closed the old man's eyes
the way he once folded the apple tree in Eden

The Birth Beneath the Tree of Eden

Silver butterfly leaves
    waving on moonlight branches

Each flap a secret lip
    interpreting God's silence

Eve rips out the rib
    and calls it husband

Lilith Leaves Eden

Hailstorms of snakes fall from the sky like apples

shatter forbidden naked ice river

swarm and moan on her helpless organs frozen beneath

She rises and rides on snakes

speeds to unknown spring

Paradise Express

After weighing it, Anubis

dips the soul into Lethe

wrings out every drop of memory

irons every crease of sorrow

wraps it in a parcel

waybill attached

    Name: Simone Weil

    Weight: Light

    Category: Saint

    Sender: Anubis

    Recipient: God

slides the box onto the conveyor belt

that conveys it all the way to the realm of light

Become a Buddha

Pray in endless reincarnation

gazing at eternity

Nirvana

Inside the Temple of Nirvana
eighty-eight death masks float

I enter the Mandala
All the masks ignite, wheeling in air

I see my reincarnations on every mask
I hear my karma crackling in the tempestuous fire

Undaunted, I walk forward with palms folded
Wheel of Samsara smashed into ashes of illusion

I rest beyond life and death

On Eternity

Eternity is not to be gained

but

became

Icarus

I shall rise from the ocean like a newborn sun

wings thrashing fiery storms

I shall soar to the most high

with infinite gold beneath

Vanitas Vanitatum Omnia Vanitas

Crows hang upside down from the dead sky

Women push the laughing babies back into holes

Men hose down the volcanic fire with sperm

Angels and demons love and bite each other

each bite an abyss

Part II

Whistled the hole
in Jesus' palm

Wind

Wind swings through my hair and whispers its story

I danced on the bodies of Job's children

I whistled the hole in Jesus' palm

I kissed the praying lips of Teresa of Ávila

Oh, wind

before you continue your eternal exile

tell me: Where have you come from?

Expelled from Eden

I am the howl of

Adam and Eve

Why Christ Was Born in a Manger

A horse chews its fate before death

whipped

iron nailed to its feet

Cross as Ultimate Unity
of Life and Death

Vertical
   Stand upright while alive

Horizonal
   Lie flat while dead

The Crucifixion

If spirit is more important than flesh

why does Jesus shoulder and suffer our sins

nails pounded into his body?

Valley of the Shadow of Death

Answer me:
Where is the valley of the shadow of death?

Is it in the shade
    beneath the eternal suffering of the cross?

Or is it within the wrinkles of my mother's face?

When I am little
she hums a lullaby
promises me immortality

but the furrows on her forehead reveal to me
    the judgment of life and death

By Cradle, By Grave

Ma!

Fingers in mouth

Ma...

Flowers in hand

Shadow Walking

I trudge with my shadow like Jesus dragging his sorrow

A dark light shoots through my heart

Opening my arms, I fall backward

a cross into an abyss

Theotokos

You arise from ashes of last sunglow

my rose of undying dreams

Annunciation

She sees the everlasting snow in the fire

She reaches out to that glowing white

Upon her touch, thorn fire flows through her fingers

stings them

Innocent blood blossoms in flame

Rose petals yearn for the dew of God

shivering open to the Ultimate

Gabriel cradles the snow

places it on the pistil

Holiness floods the flower with light

The earth trembles for the weight of a white rose

Boding Blood

By moonlight, the Virgin is sewing clothes
for the baby in her belly

She hums with joy, imagining
he will become a good carpenter

Ah! She gasps as the needle pricks her finger

Beads of blood drip and stain the cloth

like glistening wounds

Father and Son

The carpenter places his calloused palm
upon her virgin belly

The baby within loosens his fist
stretches out to connect

Old hands plane wood to provide for the family
Young hands pinned to wood will atone for humanity

Star of Bethlehem

Starlight apparition of smoke angels

A baby cries

A mother rejoices

Folks slumber

unaware of the light
streaming serenely onto their faces

Baptism of Christ

Water splashes

Firmament splits

Spirit spreads wings

Son of God stands solemn and serene

Hair dew sparkles

drips into the river

the heartbeat of eternity

Holy Butterfly

I 'light on Christ's shoulder, flapping my wings

He carries me along the thorny path of blood and flame

When I become his heavenly wings

I gaze down at my dead body

The cross stands upright

Advent of Christ

I shake off my shadow and leap to the skies

lie among prophets

We sparkle like silver feathers

The Messiah descends the celestial stairs of our souls

Banquet on the Sea

Mermaids holding candles rise from the depths
their vestal bodies covered by flaming white shells

Moonlight bakes the leviathan
Salty water washes away sin

Mermaids slice the dead beauty with shells
gorge on the innocent meat

Candles are incarnadined by splashes
Lightning tears apart the sky

The Messiah lands on that giant skeleton
a throne for the king of kings

Mermaids float in waves with bloody delicacies
spreading over their lily breasts

The candlelight on their foreheads guides the righteous
to join the sacred dinner

Last Judgment

From the hole in Christ's palm
    the nail falls into the lake

Thundering fire erupts

The colossal cross soars from the depths

Angels on clouds blow the endgame trumpets

Summoned by the sound

all the living and the dead

flutter in the air like notes composing the finale

They swirl around the luminous crucifix

see their reflections

Some, panicked by an image of a dark moth

drop into the lake of fire

Some, enraptured by an image of a niveous dove

spread their hurricane wings

All the past is swept to dust

Creation's new epoch begins

Ascension

The blood of Christ burns scarlet snow

falling like the ashes of eternity
    covering the wasteland

Earth is holy grail

Sinners and saints float and freeze
    like fleeting ants

Snow melts

Souls evaporate to heaven

Divinity Harvest

The sickle in her hand
glides through an ocean of red heads

splash splash

every rose a Jesus

Jesus' Bride

A heart, tender as a kiss on snow

the tears she shed for the poor

become pearls adorning her wedding gown

She walks down the aisle paved with angel feathers

Will the groom wait for her at the end?

Will she stretch her trembling finger
    toward that hallowed ring

toward the hollow of his palm?

Salome

Why not sink into my breasts?
Soften your search for ultimate truth

Why not entangle with my tongue?
Quench your thirst for eternal bliss

Why not kiss my feet?
Crush the path you prepare for the Nazarene

Must I savor heaven's temptation on your dead lips?

Your head
    rests in plate

My heart
    shall never rest in peace

John the Divine

Passion as paddle

belief as boat

crossing the sea of light to witness the will of God

a prisoner on Patmos

the pilgrim to Paradise

a despised exile from an ephemeral regime

the destined revelator of the eternal realm

Saint Francis of Assisi
Receiving the Stigmata

Seraph plucks five flaming feathers

Flesh is shot and penetrated

Tears drip on morning grass

Crystals bounce

Roses blossom

Joan of Arc

The maid on horseback
leaps over my fingers

hooves thumping
as I strike the keyboard

The Criminals Crucified
on Crosses Alongside Christ

Cars cruise on the fated crossroad

two kinds of drivers

criminal on the left

criminal on the right

Christ is not in either backseat

I Am

fire

fire

fire

the waving skirt of Joan of Arc

the thorny crown of Jesus Christ—

I am

coming soon

Sommo Poeta

I rest in the chant of angels

until that flaming hand awakens me

Part III

Your name is the last dew
on my withered rose lips

When I Blow with the Wind

Your name is the last dew
on my withered rose lips

Love and Eternity

You spread over me
like moonlight running on water

Buddha muses on the secret of eternity

We are in love

Secret of Heaven

Dawn rises
from your eyes

Dusk falls
into mine

Shall I unveil your
golden mask of divinity

to glance
what heaven is like?

To Alien

Raise your eyes

Search for that shyest star

and we shall kiss

just by gazing

Amazing Grace

Angel face

storm heart

through you

light expresses itself

To Love of My Life and Beyond

You drag your shadow—
    three thousand years of solitude and sorrow

You wander in the wilderness of time
    searching for the meaning of love and death

When finally we meet

as if holding eternity for the first time

I will cradle your head in my palms

Love

Flames

kissing

fire

Love Is Ultimate Redemption

A tear shed for love
is deeper than the sea

When I murmur your name to the winds
I am as clean as Yahweh's bones

Legend

Souls spiral into butterflies flying

then fall onto the river

like autumn leaves

What Is a Love

Flesh entangles

the two planks of a cross

our souls nailed

bleeding yet blazing

like blood

Love redeems

Hug

Your fingers are candles

each nail a wick

I am

fire

Leaf and Wind

I'm about to fall
She catches and carries me away
We intertwine crazily
and I think I shall never fall

Suddenly, I am on the ground alone
I curl up my body, cry over her leaving
After crying out the last drop
I dry up and die

Oh, careless stranger
when you tread on me
what you hear is the last faint crack
of my yellow broken heart

A Tree Is a Sad Skeleton of the Earth

As wind peels the last leaf off my hug

winter whistles through my empty branches

I wave and wave

A ring grows in silence

a halo for little green souls resting in the soil

Parting: A Red Sea Love Story

After long journeys

two fish finally meet

love at first sight

They are going to kiss

Suddenly, almost-joined-lips are split by Moses' waves

bodies tossed to separate shores

Mouths open and close, on and on, as if they are kissing

Not even death can do them part

Back

She is running toward you
petal toes, morning dew
shining in every step

She is running toward you
seaweed hair winds
making love on every strand

She is running toward you
colors back to the rainbow
Eve back to Adam's chest
Son of God back to mother's cradle

Ark

You swing an axe to the left and the right

My arms emerge, encircle you tight

You break the bow

My head emerges, kisses you crazy

You chop the stern right at the center

My legs emerge and split

Sweet vortex sucks you in

The flood baptizes you

The ark is smashed

I become your new Ark, new God

Angel

Your sigh

makes the moon rise

Strangers

We walked past

did not look at each other

We were in love for one moment

when our shadows overlapped

You Did Not

You did not sigh
but I heard the wind

You did not cry
but I felt the rain

You did not say a word
but I was grateful

Now when you do
speak to me

I know
I am in a dream

Cup

You empty my cup

by filling

hers

My Eyes Are Big Yet Small

Though my eyes can hold infinity

they cannot hold your tears

Blossoms

Umbrellas spread

Drops splash down, glistening on colors

We are all beautiful flowers

Divinity

Angels strip my flesh

wrap my soul with golden threads

When I emerge from the cocoon

I soar to the Divine

Desire

I undress you

cover you in my dream

just in case

you slip into others'

I Want to Dance for You

I don the ocean and twirl

The tsunami sweeps you under

Shower Tempest

Hot rain beats our skin

We hug

Thunder roars

Lightning flashes

in our bones

Taiji

O, that piano is burning

It melts and morphs into a circle

black and white

yang and yin

groom and bride

the black and white in our eyes

That piano is playing

The man in black holding hands with the woman in white—

they gaze into each other's eyes

into eternity

We Are So Beautiful

Every fleeting moment

we breathe and create together

is eternity

My Dear Dear

Every time I kiss your eye

a little flower

blossoms somewhere

unknown

Little Deer

I am the little deer in your heart

Although tiny, I kiss every corner

Little Fear

When I fall in love with you

my heart becomes fragile

a butterfly dancing happily on your tail

I just hope you don't shoo me away

Breathe

Philosophy is the breath of the brain

Poetry is the breath of the heart

Shortest Poem

Love

Find Me

I am hidden away by Jesus

The only way to find me

is love

Part IV

Mushrooms are pimples
of the earth

Spider

You hunt with your web
    the vessels of your eyes

When you first spot me
    I am already captured at its center

Lovely World

Grasses are facial hairs of the earth

Mushrooms are pimples

Fog

Woods longing for water

dewy dreams twine slumberland

Where Are the Bodies of Birds

Dead on trees

reincarnate as

leaves

Lamp

Dead starlight in crystal coffin

shines on
    my endless night of cosmic loneliness

Night Sky Is a Dark Egg

Yolk is shining

Whites are floating

moon and clouds

Cross and Star

Angels slumber on crosses

When they inhale and exhale

stars twinkle all over the firmament

Soul and Star

Stars shoot into our bodies and become souls

Navels are meteorite craters

Umbilical Cord

Ten-month building delivered

Ribbon-cutting executed

What then?

Cheers

clapping

tears

collapse

Urban Concerto

People stream the zebra crossing

replay each note of the commute
on the black and white keys

Cars thunder

Traffic lights conduct
these dull and frenetic movements

Subway

Sperm sails fast in the tunnel

Iron spine under-rumbles the drumbeat of life

Faces of every molecule on board tinted with rust

Full speed ahead to the final destination

not to fulfill a great destiny

only to survive

Office Building

Towering tombstone encased by glass-coffin lids

Living corpses sit and stare

Company epitaph is composed of their names

Lunar Craters

Poor masses circle the cross

lungs chanting

Starving to death

souls crawl the moon and gnaw

God Weeps a Galaxy

Earth

a blue tear of God

All tears

break at last

evaporate

Messiah of the Sea

Water sprays from a blowhole

One whale is spotted and speared

Others are spared

Jonah in the Cosmos

The blue whale of the universe engulfs us

Cosmic ocean splashes its limpid skin

We call the waves galaxies

Angling

Angels cast fishing lines

Rain falls

Aircraft Trail

Fly past

Sky is unzipped

Family Reunion

I eat an egg

then a hen—

together again

The Old Man and His Last Battle

Hemingway's old man sets sail for the last time

surfing on the fish bone with a spear

throws it

a bullet to the throat

The Ultimate's Game

Stars of all shapes and colors

floating across galactic boards

We Are Not Forgotten

God always pays the electricity bill

That's why the moon shines every night

Revelation

Epicurus:

Is God willing to prevent evil but not able?
Then he is not omnipotent

Is he able but not willing?
Then he is malevolent

Is he both able and willing?
Then whence cometh evil?

Is he neither able nor willing?
Then why call him God?

Xueyan:

God never
needs us to call

God's Boredom

In the bedroom beyond

God, bored, bores a hole in a box

Humans inside cheer at the opening

What a beautiful bright moon!

Moon Breasts

Curtain of night slides

A pair of full moons appear

shimmering, demure, ivory white

Only a lonely fool would rather land on
that cold old revolving rock

in a fuck-away universe

Cigarette

Baby cake never smokes

I put a candle in its mouth and light

When I blow out the candle

it is grownup

then ground up by my teeth

To Wake

Humans wake because they are hungry

not because they love the world

Xueyan's Confession

Breaking free from waves of sorrows
I leap ashore

Stars coronate me
beads of tears on hairs ribboned by light

I am owned by eternity

雪雁

Xueyan lives in China. She was born August 8, 1993.

Acknowledgments

Thanks to the editors of the following journals for publishing these poems:

"Ark" - *Ginosko Literary Journal*
"Cup" - *The Bangalore Review*
"Desire" - *Ginosko Literary Journal*
"Divinity" - *Ginosko Literary Journal*
"Fog" - *Ginosko Literary Journal*
"I Want to Dance for You" - *Ginosko Literary Journal*
"Jesus' Bride" - *Ginosko Literary Journal*
"My Eyes Are Big Yet Small" - *The Bangalore Review*
"Shower Tempest" - *Ginosko Literary Journal*
"Strangers" - *Ginosko Literary Journal*
"Taiji" - *Ginosko Literary Journal*
"To Alien" - *The Bangalore Review*

Title Index

X

Y

First Line Index

B

C

D

E

F

Y

CPSIA information can be obtained
at www.ICGtesting.com
Printed in the USA
BVHW042241291222
655301BV00010B/347